Roger Coote and Diana Bentley

My
Big Brother

Firefly

My brother is older than me.
He's a teenager.
He's taller than I am and when
my ball was stuck in a tree . . .

. . . my big brother climbed up and got it for me.

One of my brother's friends has
a very big dog.
It's bigger than me.

My brother and his friends do
lots of things together.

They go dancing . . .

. . . and play team games.

They do their homework . . .

. . . and go to school together.

But sometimes my brother looks lonely and sad.

My mum says teenagers
feel sad sometimes . . .

. . . but at other times they are happy.

My friend has a big sister.
Here he is with his family.

Do you have a big sister or
a big brother?

Notes for adults

Children who go to school already knowing how a book 'works' have a great deal of knowledge that will help them to make the entry into reading much easier. It is far more important to share a book with a child than to try to teach him/her to read. These Firefly books aim to introduce very young children to the world around them.

Before reading this book talk about the pictures on the cover. What does your child think the book is about? Talk about the title and point to the words. Tell him/her that all books are written by authors and often illustrated by a different person. Show him/her the names of the author and illustrator.

Before reading the story look through the book together and talk about the illustrations. If you wish, you can use the discussion points below, or make up your own questions. Encourage the child to tell his/her own story to the pictures. This important pre-reading skill helps children to develop an understanding of story that is essential to reading. Do let your child hold the book and give him/her time to look at the pictures before talking about them. Adults often rush in with questions far too soon.

Remember, when discussing the pictures there is no 'right' or 'wrong' guess. Accept what your child suggests and add your own ideas. You will be bringing much more knowledge to the pictures but s/he may surprise you.

After reading the book let your child explore the book on his/her own. S/he may want to return to a favourite picture, retell the story to a special toy, or just turn the pages pretending to be a reader. A joy in books comes from the reader being allowed to use them as s/he wishes and not necessarily in what an adult thinks is the 'right' way.

Discussion points

Talking about the illustrations will help your child to get more from the story. Here are some suggestions for things to discuss. The numbers refer to the pages on which the illustrations appear.

5	Can you see the ball in the tree? What do you think the little girl is saying to her brother?
7	Can you climb trees?
9	What time of year is it in the picture?
11	Where are the people exploring? What are they carrying?
12/13	What are these people doing? Do you think they are having fun?
15	Which side do you think is winning the game? Does the dog want to play?
17	Who is peeping round the door? What can they see?
18/19	What do you think these people are talking about? Why is the dog running?
21	Why do you think the boy looks sad?
23	What do you think the people are waiting for?
24/25	How many people can you count?
27	Do you like swinging? What have the boys been playing?